Opera Cats

Opera Cats

Susan Herbert

THAMES AND HUDSON

FRONTISPIECE:

Der Rosenkavalier

ACT II

At the suggestion of his lover, the Marschallin, Count Octavian presents the silver rose to the young Sophie on behalf of the aging roué, Baron Ochs.

British Library Cataloguing-in-Publication Data
A catalogue record for this book is available
from the British Library
ISBN 0-500-01805-7
Printed and bound in Hong Kong by C&C Offset

OPPOSITE:

Turandot

ACT III

All the potential suitors of the cruel Princess Turandot have been executed for failing to answer her impossible riddles. Prince Calef succeeded, but, because he loved the Princess, he gave her a chance to escape him if she could guess his name. Now he has told her his name at the risk of his own life, and she suddenly realises that she loves him in return.

Aida

ACT II

Returning victorious from defeating the Ethiopians, Radames is informed by the King that he is to marry Amneris. As Radames is in love with Aida, daughter of the Ethiopian king, Amonasro, this is not good news.

The Magic Flute

ACT I

Prince Tamino, fleeing from a savage dragon, collapses unconscious.
Meanwhile, the three ladies, attendants of the Queen of the Night,
vanquish the dragon and cast admiring eyes over the Prince.

The Magic Flute
ACT II

*The vengeful Queen of the Night
gives her daughter a dagger,
and orders her to kill the High Priest, Sarastro.*

Die Fledermaus

ACT II

During his lavish party, Prince Orlovsky drinks a toast to the king of wines, champagne. The party is serving as a setting for Dr Falke to take his long overdue revenge on his friend Gabriel von Eisenstein. To aid him in his plot, Falke has invited to the party Eisenstein's maid, Adele, disguised as an actress, and his wife Rosalinda, disguised as a Hungarian countess.

Madame Butterfly
ACT II

After marrying the fifteen-year-old Cio-Cio San, Lt Pinkerton has returned to the USA. Although he has been away for three years, Cio-Cio San still believes that he will return. Her maid, Suzuki, has her doubts.

La Traviata

ACT I

*Alfredo Germont is taken to a party at the house of Violetta Valery, a beautiful courtesan,
whom Alfredo has loved from afar for more than a year.*

La Traviata

ACT II

Violetta has left Alfredo at the behest of his father. Believing her to have returned to her lover,
Douphol, of her own free will, Alfredo catches up with her at Flora's gambling party,
and insults her by throwing his winnings in her face.

Così fan Tutte

ACT I

The cynical Don Alfonso persuades his young friends, Ferrando and Guglielmo, to test the fidelity of their fiancées, Fiordiligi and Dorabella. Having pretended to go off to war, the two young men return disguised as Albanians and each attempts to win the affections of the other's sweetheart.
At first, the two ladies will have nothing to do with them,
so the 'Albanians' pretend to take poison.

Pagliacci

ACT I

Canio, the leader of the strolling players,
has discovered that his wife Nedda is being unfaithful to him.
He sadly laments that he must don his make-up and
play the clown when his heart is breaking.

Das Rheingold

SCENE II

The giants Fasolt and Fafner have built the palace Valhalla for Wotan.
Wotan unwisely agreed to give them Freia, the goddess of youth, as their payment,
intending to find something else for them before payment was due.
This he has failed to do, in spite of Loge's help,
so the giants drag Freia away, refusing to return her unless
Wotan is able to get them Alberich's gold.

Das Rheingold
SCENE III

Having stolen the magic gold from the Rhinemaidens, Alberich makes himself Lord of the World, and exercises his power by forcing the other Nibelungs to obey him. Wotan and Loge, who have descended into Nibelheim with the intention of robbing Alberich of the gold, look on with interest and await their opportunity.

Siegfried

ACT I

The young Siegfried has forged his new sword, Nothung,
from the broken remains of his father Siegmund's weapon. Mime, the Nibelung,
kept the remains of the sword hidden, when he found Siegfried's mother Sieglinde dying in the forest,
having just given birth. Mime has raised Siegfried, in the hope that his mighty strength
will be enough to vanquish Fafner, who has transformed himself into a dragon
and is the current holder of the Ring.

Boris Godunov

PROLOGUE

Russia is suffering, and the people long for a new tsar who will bring peace and justice.
Boris Godunov has been crowned with full ceremony. However, he has a bad
conscience, since he was responsible for the death of Dmitry,
the son of the previous tsar Ivan the Terrible.

Eugene Onegin

ACT II

At a party, Eugene Onegin deliberately
provokes his friend Lensky by flirting outrageously with Lensky's beloved, Olga.
Lensky challenges Onegin to a duel, and Onegin kills him.

Tosca

ACT II

To save the life of her beloved Cavaradossi,
Tosca has agreed to spend the night with Scarpia, the chief of police.
Once the order of release is signed, Tosca stabs the evil Scarpia to death.

Die Walküre

ACT III

After the death of Siegmund and Hunding, Brünnhilde rescues Sieglinde, against her father's orders.
She appeals to the other Valkyries to shield her from Wotan's rage.

Die Walküre

ACT III

Despite Brünnhilde's pleading, Wotan is determined to punish her by depriving her of her supernatural status and putting her to sleep, to be defenceless against the first man who wakes her. However, to ensure that only a hero will be able to do this, he agrees to surround her with a ring of fire. Then he bids her a sad farewell.

Tristan und Isolde

ACT I

Tristan is taking the Princess Isolde back to Cornwall, as a bride for King Mark.
They are deeply in love, though neither has admitted this to the other.
Isolde plans a suicide pact with poisoned wine, but before they drink,
Isolde's maid Brangane substitutes a love potion for the poison.
By the time they arrive in Cornwall, Tristan and Isolde are
irrevocably besotted.

Die Meistersinger von Nürnberg

ACT III

Walther von Stolzing sings his Prize Song
before the assembled mastersingers. Walther has no
wish to become a mastersinger himself, but he has
fallen in love with Eva (who is the prize), and the
kindly cobbler-poet, Hans Sachs, has helped
him to create his winning song.

Don Giovanni

ACT II

The libertine, Don Giovanni, having killed Donna Anna's father,
mocks the dead man's statue in the churchyard and makes the mistake of inviting it to dinner.
He is considerably alarmed when the statue arrives to keep the appointment.

The Marriage of Figaro
ACT IV

Count Almaviva begs forgiveness of his Countess.
He has been foiled in his pursuit of Susanna
(Figaro's betrothed) by the Countess and Susanna
exchanging dresses and wearing masks.

Fidelio

ACT I

Leonora and Jaquino open the doors of the State Prison, and all the prisoners emerge into the light. Leonora is disguised as Fidelio, and she is trying to find out the whereabouts of her husband Florestan, who has been wrongfully imprisoned by the evil Pizarro.

Cavalleria Rusticana

The peasant girl Santuzza has been jilted by her lover Turridu, who has returned to his former love, Lola, although she is now married to Alfio. Santuzza has been excommunicated, and laments her lot while everyone else files into the church on Easter Sunday.

Lucia di Lammermoor

ACT III

Enrico forces his sister Lucia into marriage with Arturo,
knowing that she is really in love with Edgardo.
On her wedding night, Lucia stabs her new husband
to death, and then goes completely off her head.

Faust

ACT III

Faust, having sold his soul to Mephistopheles,
has regained his youth. He woos the chaste
young Marguerite in her garden,
while Mephistopheles looks on.

Rigoletto

ACT II

Gilda, the daughter of the jester Rigoletto, has been abducted by the Duke of Mantua's courtiers. The Duke, who has been wooing Gilda on the quiet, disguised as a student, no sooner finds her in his own palace than he seduces her. Her father comforts her in her shame and despair, and swears vengeance on the Duke.

The Barber of Seville

ACT I

The barber, Figaro, recounts the many reasons why he is indispensable to everyone in Seville. He is about to assist the young Count Almaviva in his pursuit of Rosina, who is kept confined to the house by her guardian, Dr Bartolo.

Susan Herbert

Carmen

ACT IV

*The fickle Carmen, having transferred her affections from
the disgraced corporal, Don Jose, to the toreador, Escamillo,
rejects the pleas of her former lover outside the bull-ring.
In a fit of jealous rage and despair, Don Jose kills her.*

La Bohème

ACT II

The four friends (poet, composer, painter, philosopher) and their neighbour Mimi have an evening out at the Café Momus. Their enjoyment is interrupted by the arrival of Musetta and her elderly lover, Alcindoro. Musetta is the former love of the painter Marcello, and while Alcindoro studies the menu, Musetta seeks to draw Marcello back into her net

La Bohème

ACT IV

Some time after parting from her lover, Rodolfo, the seamstress Mimi arrives at his attic home, in the last stages of consumption. Everyone rallies round to help; Musetta fetches her muff for the ailing Mimi, and the philosopher Colline pawns his old overcoat to buy medicine for her. But it is too late, and Mimi dies soon after her arrival.